Designer Scrapbooks

with Susan Rios

Designer Scrapbooks
with Susan Rios

Sterling Publishing Cc. Inc., New York
A Sterling/Chapelle Book

Chapelle, Ltd., Inc., P.O. Box 9252, Ogden, UT 84409
  (801) 621-2777 • (801) 621-2788 Fax
  e-mail: chapelle@chapelleltd.com
  Web site: www.chapelleltd.com

A Red Lips 4 Courage book
  Red Lips 4 Courage Communications, Inc.
  8502 E. Chapman Ave., 303
  Orange, CA 92869
  Web site: www.redlips4courage.com

Library of Congress Cataloging-in-Publication Data

Rios, Susan.
  Designer scrapbooks with Susan Rios.
    p. cm.
  Includes index.
  ISBN 1-4027-2034-3
  1. Photograph albums. 2.   Photographs--Conservation and
restoration. 3.   Scrapbooks. I. Title.

TR465.R56 2005
745.593--dc22

                                              2005012694

10 9 8 7 6 5 4 3 2 1
Published by Sterling Publishing Co., Inc.
387 Park Ave. South, New York, NY 10016
©2005 Susan Rios, Inc.
Distributed in Canada by Sterling Publishing
c/o Canadian Manda Group, 165 Dufferin St.
Toronto, Ontario, Canada M6K 3H6
Distributed in Great Britain by Chrysalis Books Group PLC,
The Chrysalis Building,
Bramley Road, London W10 6SP, England
Distributed in Australia by Capricorn Link (Australia) Pty. Ltd.
P. O. Box 704, Windsor, NSW 2756, Australia
Printed and Bound in China
All Rights Reserved

Sterling ISBN No. 1-4027-2034-3

For information about custom editions, special sales, premium
and corporate purchases, please contact Sterling Special Sales
Department at 800-805-5489 or specialsales@sterlingpub.

Foreword

Facing the Fear of Art

Being an artist and not specifically a scrapbooker, I'm really proud of this book. Learning as I went along, I feel I bring a unique perspective to the concept of scrapbooking, which is, anyone who wants to do it can, and you can make beautiful and unique pages of your own.

You don't necessarily have to go out and buy everything, as many of the things I used to embellish my pages were things I already had: vintage valentines and postcards, old laces and trims, flowers, buttons, and items cut out of my own artwork.

Save beautiful greeting cards and Christmas cards, and cut up old magazines when you see something you like. So many things can by used, and as you go along, you will develop an "eye" for spotting and saving things that appeal to you to later incorporate into your scrapbook pages. I would even encourage you to create some papers of your own. I bought plain paper of different colors and hand painted them. You could paint something as simple as polka dots, stripes, stars, or flowers in the color palette you desire for a particular page.

Whenever I teach art workshops, one of the biggest challenges students face is the fear of art; that they can't create, or things won't be "good enough." Well, I'm here to tell you that not being good enough is a challenge for every artist, on every level.

I invite you to put your fear aside, along with all of the negative things you have told yourself for so long, and begin to appreciate your own uniqueness in a new way. Much success in life is first believing you can do it, and then doing it.

My biggest hope is that you will approach this book with new eyes, put on your own "artist's hat," and draw inspiration from my work, to incorporate into yours.

Susan Rios

Contents

Introduction

An Artist's Humble Beginnings

Having been a professional artist for nearly three decades, I am a very visual person. Through my art, I create images that people almost always connect with on an emotional level. Many times I'm creating imaginary places where I would like to be.

"I want to walk down that path, or stroll through that garden," or, "I want to sit in that chair and enjoy the view," are things I often hear about my paintings when I meet people at art shows. It is very satisfying to listen to what people have to say about my work.

Because of my career, I've met lovely and amazing people and have formed endearing friendships, and I have been very touched by the impact my work has had on so many others.

I always say I feel more like a native Californian with good Midwest values.

Early Snapshots

I was born in Terre Haute, Indiana in 1950 and our family moved to Southern California when I was 3.

I grew up in the San Fernando Valley, a suburb of Los Angeles, with my parents and my younger sister, along with an assortment of pets including dogs, cats, hamsters, rabbits, lizards, horned toads, fish, frogs, and anything else we could convince our dad to let us keep. Our mom, being an animal lover herself, was always on our side.

My School of Life

Early on, I realized that I was good at art. I consider it a gift, because it is something I've just always been good at. In junior high school I became obsessed with horses and I drew them all the time. I had books and models of horses, and my parents let me take riding lessons once a week. Those Wednesday afternoons were heaven to me. I also started sketching stylized horses, standing dressed and on their hind legs. They had names

like Marlon Brand-O and Zsa Zsa Ga-Horse. I won an art scholarship when I was in eighth grade for a summer program at a local university.

In high school I started doing very detailed pen-and-ink drawings of imaginary creatures, which my mother dubbed "Imagimenagerie." I was on the yearbook staff throughout high school and designed the yearbook covers and many of the illustrations. I was voted "Best Artist" in my senior year.

After I graduated high school, I tried college for a while, but I wasn't really committed to it. For me, the "School of Life" has always been my best teacher, so after a few part-time jobs, I started working full time in a flower shop. I actually started out making 50 cents an hour while I learned floral design! I loved working with flowers and I was good at it. My favorite things to make were bridal bouquets because they were the most special, one-of-a-kind arrangements.

At one point I left floral design and went to work for a small advertising company in North Hollywood, California. I learned how to design and paste up ads for clients. I even learned how to hand set type, as this was before the advent of computers. I did the design, layout, and paste up of a book my employer wrote about printing. One of my favorite jobs was for a client who wanted me to design souvenir items using Smokey the Bear. I got very good at drawing Old Smokey.

My mother enjoyed dressing my younger sister and me alike.

We were Daddy's girls, and he was outnumbered by living and make-believe dolls.

Starting a Career as an Artist

If there is a recurring theme in my life, it is independence and freedom to do what I want. I realized I was not happy being the only employee at the advertising company, doing jobs that I found less than interesting. So I returned to floral design and managing the flower shop.

It was after the birth of my daughter, Olivia, that I started my career as an artist. My husband and I agreed that I would be a stay-at-home mom, but staying at home with my beautiful daughter, I questioned who I was, what was I doing, and what I had to give my child.

Around that time a friend came to dinner, saw a couple of paintings in our home, and was impressed. He later told me he thought I really had talent and offered to help me "do some-

thing with it." I went out and talked to people and sold my work myself. My friend really helped me understand the business side of art and how to set and reach goals—something I'd never learned how to do until then.

My husband and I would sell my work at sidewalk art shows, which gave me the confidence to approach galleries, and that is how I had my first one-woman show in Beverly Hills. It's also how I met my first art publisher.

I enjoyed being able to paint and work at home in the early years of my daughter's childhood.

The Spirit that Moves Me

I sold my paintings at sidewalk art shows and took orders for commissioned pieces, and learned the best and biggest lesson I've ever learned: Do not listen to people who tell you that you can't do something. Just go ahead and do it. I went ahead and did it . . . very successfully.

Going out and selling my artwork was a very scary endeavor. When you put your creative works out for public viewing it is allowing yourself to be vulnerable. This is not a comfortable feeling. My art is an expression of who I am, and the sensitivity that allows me to create and feel wonderful when it's going well is the same sensitivity that can cause me to feel inadequate when I judge myself, and what I create, as not good enough.

When I had my first one-woman show I had a panic attack. Although most people assume you can't be creative unless "the spirit moves you," I've painted through anxiety, sadness, depression, and even apathy. The satisfying part about this endurance is knowing I can get through just about anything and be OK.

For so many of us who grew up in households that were less than harmonious, we've had to face adulthood with a rather shaky foundation. By facing adversity, and getting through it, we can actually create a foundation of strength for ourselves by simply moving through it and doing our best.

People always assume that my life must be like my paintings: tranquil, serene, happy, and peaceful. Sometimes it's because I've experienced the opposite that I'm creating what I don't always have. I create life as I would like it to be, and much of the time, now it is.

I have always enjoyed meeting the people who collect my work. Their warmth and encouragement are a great inspiration. Here I am at one of my earlier art shows.

Gallery shows keep me busy and prevent me from feeling isolated. I have to spend quiet time alone in my studio to create each painting. Shows help me feel connected to other people.

Family First

When my daughter was 6, I became a single mom. I worked hard because I needed to make a living and I knew that a career as an artist was what I wanted. It's always been an amazing thing to me that I can take a blank canvas, create something unique to all the world, and have people appreciate it enough to buy it. Also, I have always had the mindset that I would succeed.

I have been able to have a home-based career that enabled me to be a stay-at-home mom. School plays, PTA meetings, and time with my daughter were more important to me than any painting I could have ever done.

From Businesswoman Back to Artist

Being with a major art publisher for 10 years, my paintings became known internationally. A book of my work was published during this time and I did shows in galleries across the country. When that relationship ended, I decided to self-publish my work and for five years I ran The Susan Rios Company. While I grew my company, it was at the sacrifice of "being" the artist, so I took another direction.

It is true that when one door closes another one opens. Once I let go of running a company I managed to connect with the person who helped me create the new business I had envisioned. Greg Johnsen and I started Susan Rios Inc.

Greg's business background and expertise allows him to run the company from our offices in Sherman Oaks, California, which permits me to be the artist. We are business partners, great friends, and I can't imagine life without him. In addition to fine art, my work is licensed and appears on a variety of products such as books, calendars, puzzles, needlepoint, and stationery.

Putting this book together has been an interesting and satisfying experience, and has broadened my creative horizons in many ways. I've always kept scrapbooks and have loved recording memorable events in my life. It really took me awhile to get into the pages without that critical inner judge. By not comparing myself, and exploring my own ideas, I started to have fun creating my pages, and I hope you do too.

My studio is my sanctuary and the place where I take joy in solitude and creativity.

13

I am so fortunate to be able to follow my artistic passion and make my living doing what I love.

Indulging in Passions

Many of my scrapbook papers were created using flowers from my paintings. I made hand-painted papers when I wanted a certain look, and for the Night Before Christmas pages I used a copy of an actual painting for the paper.

My favorite part was indulging in my love of vintage materials and using them with my own papers to create the look I wanted. I have a collection of vintage valentines, many of which I cut up and used throughout the book. I collect old buttons, lace, ribbons, trims, and millenary flowers and I searched the Internet to find more for these scrapbook pages. I used vintage lace as background elements and with my computer I scanned old handkerchiefs, which I then printed out to use as borders. I love combining all of these elements to enhance the photos and to fashion a soft look on the pages.

Finding Your Way

Creating scrapbook pages has to do with remembering and honoring someone, or something, important in your life. It is personal and should be recorded that way. Just like any form of art, there is no "right" or "wrong" way to do it. There is just "your" way.

Being a self-taught painter, I learned how to do scrapbook pages based on what I wanted to say, or how I wanted something to feel. This book became a labor of love, to honor the people and the memories I cherish. I let the events and the people in the photos guide me in putting the pages together. I think my pages reflect who I am.

It is my hope that this book will not only be a source of inspiration and ideas, but it will help liberate your "artist within."

Scrapbooking is a wonderful way to incorporate things you adore with photographs you treasure. It's also a great excuse to collect more of what you love, and the more you do, the more inspired you become. Set your creative spirit free, and let your scrapbook pages reflect the canvas of your life.

Special places are often my inspiration. A favorite inn to visit, "Tea at Summer Hill" takes me back to that Southern California seaside town I love.

SusanRios

Techniques

Making Your Own Papers

Making your own scrapbooking papers is actually fairly simple. One of the biggest challenges facing scrapbookers is having the right paper for the right project. The technology is out there; it's just knowing where to look and how to use it once you have found it. The five key elements needed to create your own 12" x 12" paper include:

- 13" x 13" paper
- Computer with image editing software
- Large-format printer
- Paper trimmer
- Scanner

Scanning Artwork

The big quest is finding paper large enough to print on. The minimum dimension to produce a 12" paper is 13". This allows the printer a half-inch margin on either side. Paper sized to 13" x 19" will be the easiest to find. I suggest you locate a store that focuses on paper products, or check on-line for paper suppliers. You may have to special order the paper, but the right paper will allow you to produce the look you want. Once you are set up with the equipment, the process rolls right along.

When you have selected your fabric, paper, or some other material, place it on the bed of the scanner, right side down, and scan at a higher dpi (I find that 300 dpi works well). There may be times you will have to make two separate scans if the item is too big. That's where the image editing software comes in handy. Using the software, you can merge both images, created by your two scans, into one. This may take some trial and error but the help guides in the software are useful.

Once you have the image merged, you can now edit it any way you want. Change the color, increase the transparency, or even add text to it. When you are satisfied with the image, it is time for sizing and printing. Some editing software allows you to change the size of an image within the program. But sometimes seeing it on the paper is easier. I like to use Adobe Page Maker for laying out background papers (and even pages themselves). With Page Maker (or other publishing software) you can set your paper size (13" x 19") and place your background image in just the right place and size you desire. It's a wonderful tool for custom scrapbooking. With that done, send to print, and trim paper to the proper size.

(Opposite page) Feel free to scan my hand-painted page and use it on your own projects.

I copied a portion of one of my paintings for a particular paper, but you can also paint your own papers.

Using too many layers of paper can make pages bulky, so I often scan the layers to design one sheet of paper. Here I scanned two papers to create one background sheet.

Painting Papers

There are multiple ways of making other papers to suit your needs as you design your memory pages. One technique used many times throughout this book is painting. A heavy cardstock paper should be used so that there is minimal warping after paint is applied and as it dries. Any regular acrylic paint right out of the tube works. This technique is perfect for those scrapbook artists who have experience with tole painting, tromp l'oeil, or even stenciling.

After your custom painted paper has dried, set it between a stack of heavy books to help the paper relax. Lay books flat so that you have a smooth surface to work with. If you don't want to use the actual paper, this is a perfect opportunity to scan your custom paper, make a digital image, and print it.

Layering Papers

Often, I layer several papers to create a fuller background for my memory pages; but using five or six papers just for the background can get bulky at times. This situation calls for digitally scanning patterns and papers. Today's computer programs allow you to do much of the assembly work first and then print it on one sheet of paper. This leaves your pages lightweight, while allowing you to achieve the depth of multiple papers for the background.

I enjoy creating my own hand-painted papers. My love for vintage things—buttons, pearls, ribbons, and even valentines—inspired many scrapbook pages throughout this book.

Sources for Vintage Charm

As you will see I have a great affinity for vintage things. Lace, ribbons, and doilies all bring back the richness of memorable times gone by. If you don't have your own items on hand, finding these things can be a chore.

I have discovered that the Internet is one of the best places to locate wonderful vintage materials for your scrapbooks. There are many on-line auction websites in which people are willing to part with these precious items. Using key words like "vintage," "old," and "antique" can help narrow your search.

Reference books on vintage collectable items are also available. Such books have helped guide me in my quest for a genuine vintage feel or giving a newer piece an old look. A reference book with prices helps you know if you are getting a bargain.

I find that looking for that special piece of lace or silk can be fun but time consuming. Be careful not to spend too much time looking or you won't have time for creating your pages!

Layering Tiers of Images

One of the things I love about creating scrapbook pages is that there are no limits on how you can design your pages. One of the best ways to be creative is to add dimension and texture.

One of my favorite techniques is tiering, or layering, images. I like to take several copies of one photograph and then carefully cut a portion of each one, stacking each part and adhering with foam tape to create incredible depth and interest. One of my favorite projects using this technique is the Rose Tea table tray. I used several copies of my painting, The Rose Room (pictured here), and cut each copy according to what depth they were in the painting. Outside the windows would be the first layer, the interior windows and walls the second, the couch the third, and the table the fourth. You can make it as simple or complex as you like. Just be sure that you use very sharp scissors and a fine-tip craft knife to ensure that your cuts are clean.

Layering isn't just for big projects or pictures. Anything can be used, including a photograph, sticker, flower, or photocopied lace. This is one technique that you can let your imagination be your guide.

With a good pair of scissors or a craft knife you can cut out certain portions of multiple copies of an image and adhere them in layers using foam squares.

Dimensional Paint

Dimensional paint is my newest love for enhancing scrapbook pages. It has the versatility and durability to do almost anything you wish. With a fine assortment of tips and colors you can embellish your pages with writing, add dimensional edges, or even create memory book gingerbread houses, as you will see in Chapter Six.

Texture medium can be applied directly onto cardstock pages or you can pre-make your designs on wax paper and then attach after they dry with craft glue.

Dimensional paint is easy to use and has many applications. One of my favorite treatments is to add vintage mica glitter before it dries. This technique looks especially nice on holiday wraps.

Texture medium can be used to make decorative objects too. Here I created a small snowman and a colorful tree by using a number of different decorating tips.

Chapter One

Family Memories

It seems to me that scrapbooking was born out of the many photographs we all have of family. I loved working on these pages, especially the one celebrating my parents' wedding. I used many vintage elements, like my grandmother's handkerchiefs, to create things like the border around a picture. I also hand painted the forget-me-not paper behind one photo to go with old valentines I used on a page.

So many things from your family's past can be used to embellish your pages: trims from an old wedding dress, a snip of a veil, lace hankies, flowers, a small pin, and a stray pearl can all be adhered right onto a page, or photographed or scanned into a computer then printed, cut out, and glued to the page.

Our Family 1996

Victorian Portrait
Beloved family members take center stage on this scrapbook page, where a large family portrait is surrounded by silk and velvet accents. I enjoy mixing vintage ribbons, flowers, and other elements with copies of hand-painted floral details.

Valentine Love
Sometimes being a pack rat comes in handy. An old valentine
saved from years past serves as the title on this lovely page.
Here is an example of where I hand painted a paper and
scanned it to create the background for a page.

The
Colors
of
Love

Tabletop Canvas Frame Project

Often, scrapbook pages have deep dimensions and are too beautiful to tuck within the covers of an album. You can easily create a folding tabletop frame that will nicely display two pages by joining two artist canvases with hinges.

For a more manageable size for table display, I like to work with 8" x 10" canvases because traditional 12" x 12" pages side by side are a bit too large for my taste.

Materials
• Acid-free adhesive
• Hot glue gun
• Two 8" x 10" artist canvases stretched over wood frame
• Two small cabinet hinges

Instructions
Lay the two canvases face down and side by side, with the two inside edges as close to each other as possible. Place each cabinet hinge face down with one flap on either canvas. Place one hinge 2" from the top of the canvases and the other 2" from the bottom. Adhere each hinge flap to the canvas with the hot glue gun. If you prefer, you may use strong, quick-drying household glue. Your scrapbook pages can be attached to the frame with an adhesive of your choice. If you use a removable adhesive you will be able to easily change the pages on display.

Tabletop Canvas Frame
Hinging two canvases together creates a wonderful standing frame for displaying dimensional scrapbook pages.

When I
Turned
Fifty

50th Birthday Corset
I try to greet life's passages with a sense of humor, and
my 50th birthday provided the perfect reason for a tea
with a twist. This laced-up corset opens to reveal
memories of the day.

Personal Papers

The birthday corset page is a good example of how attractive custom papers can be. The lining of the corset is made by placing vintage lace over a mauve paper and scanning the image. The other papers used on this page were made by scanning motifs from some of my paintings and printing them out as scrapbook paper.

You can achieve the same look by using wallpaper samples. Outdated wallpaper books are available from many dealers, and they can hold good options for scrapbooking. Just be aware that the papers may not be acid free and you may want to be careful about using copies of your photos rather than originals.

Black hooks and eyes are attached to the opening of the corset design using thin satin ribbon. The same ribbon is laced through the fasteners to hold the top of the corset closed. I enjoy surprises and try to incorporate as many as I can into the design of my pages.

(Above and top right) The corset unlaces and the invitation to the party can be removed.

The Annual Gathering of Artists this Millennium year is celebrating the

50th Birthday Celebration
of
Susan Rios

Sunday,
February 13, 2000
at 11:00am
through the rest
of the day at Susan's

Please bring
something creatively
edible for the potluck!

Still
creative
after
all
these
years!

(Left) For the invitation, I found the body I wanted in a lingerie catalog ad and replaced the model's face with my own. I shared my dream body with my guests by making picks with the image on them and tucking them into the floral arrangements at my party.

These Boots are Made for Walkin' - to My Party!

Victorian Laced Boot

The Victorian boots are a natural accompaniment to the
corset. Choose simple patterns that can be filled with papers
cut into shapes. Clip art books are a good source for patterns.

My Wonderful 50th Birthday Tea
All my artist friends came, and I had Two Gorgeous Birthday Cakes!
The Best is Yet to Come...
These Boots are Made for Walkin' to My Party!

Victorian Unlaced Boot

The boot has three flaps that open, and each reveals memories of a special day. In addition to using photos, I like to include journal entries detailing my memories of the occasion.

Victorian Boot Project

The same concept of making this Victorian boot may be applied to many different images. The trick is to choose four to five basic shapes within the image and assign each one a decorative paper. Look for patterns in coloring books or clip art collections.

Materials
- ¹⁄₁₆" hole punch
- ⅛" lavender ribbon
- Cardstock, dark lavender
- Cardstock, light lavender
- Craft glue
- Decorative edge scissors
- Eight hook-and-eye sets
- Floral paper, blue and white
- Floral paper, lavender and white
- Pencil
- Scallop edge scissors
- Small rose patterned paper
- White pearl seed beads

Instructions
Using the pattern on page 33, copy at 140% twice on white paper. Trace pattern on cardstock to create your base. Using second copy, cut out individual patterns on corresponding paper. Let your imagination go wild, but the basic shoe and folds need to stay the same.

Once you have the individual pieces cut out and the shapes traced, glue them to your base. Using the hole punch, create a series of holes up to the top of the foot for lacing. Tie off with ribbon. For the folds in the boot, apply only hooks from hook-and-eye combos along the right edges. This will be the lace closure for the boot album.

Add pearl beads and floral embellishments along the edges to give this boot Victorian charm.

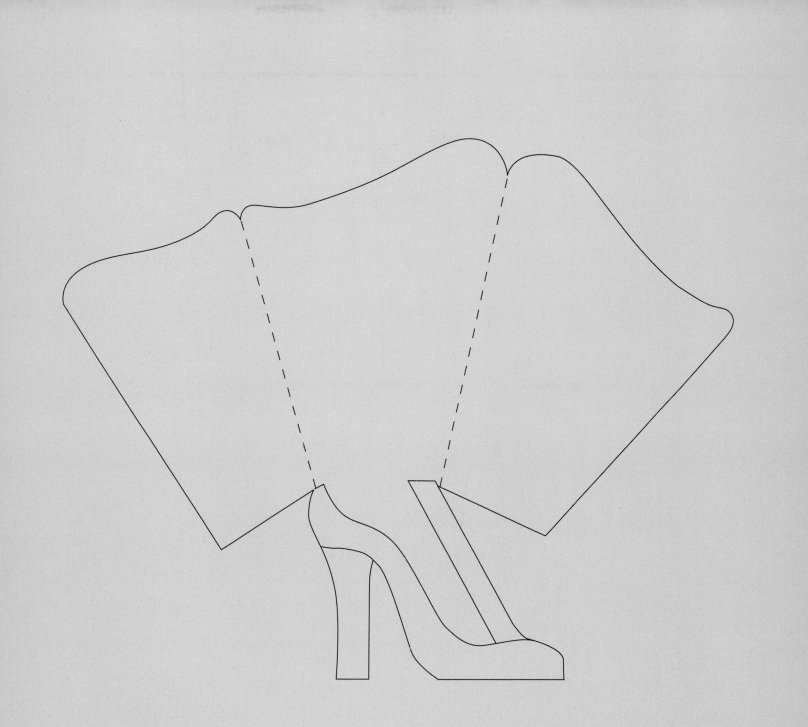

Victorian Boot Pattern

Mother-Daughter Tea
I cherish the moments I spent with my daughter, Olivia, when she was growing up. To create the fold-back opening on this page, I cut a large X with a craft knife, folded the flaps back, and lined the inside of each one with decorative paper.

Olivia + I having

Tea at Rose tree

Tea

My Beautiful Olivia, Rosemary, and Me 1995

Tea for Three

Pages can be as simple or as complex as you desire. Always keep in mind the most important thing . . . your cherished memories should be the focus of the page. The size and orientation of a fold-back opening changes based on the dimension of the opening.

Family Tree
This two-page family tree brings my family together in a symbolic way. Scanned lace cradles the portraits in the paper boughs. You can also use paper doilies as mats.

SUSAN

OLIVIA

ROSEMARY

Family Tree

Chapter Two

Partners in Play

The source of ideas for these pages was born out of a child's interests. My granddaughter, Rosie, loved wearing crowns and being the "Princess Rosebud" when she was younger. My nephew, Adam, was The Great Magician, and my daughter, Olivia, was the dancer in love with pink satin toe shoes and the grace and beauty of dance.

Children are often the inspiration for my paintings, and are featured in many of the scenes I create. Each child has something unique and special that deserves to be acknowledged and celebrated. Use that rich imagination to spark your own sense of play as you create pages that make the beloved children in your life know how truly wonderful they are.

Baby's Christening

One of my favorite memories is buying my granddaughter's christening gown, and I wanted to preserve that moment on a scrapbook page. Obviously the dress would not fit the page, so I did the next best thing. I carefully draped fabric and ribbon to create a miniature gown in the spirit of the original. Rows of thin satin ribbon mimic pin tucking.

Rosemary Elizabeth Ross

Christening Day 1994

Haircut

Tooth

Baby's First

Here We Grow

Scrapbooking is more than saving portraits; it's preserving memories of special events. Embellished matchbook boxes recall special times, like a baby's first tooth or a lock of hair from the first haircut.

Princess Rosebud

Scrapbook pages don't always need to be tucked away in a book, but rather displayed and shared every day. Since I have so many pictures of my granddaughter, Rosie, wearing crowns it was only fitting to make her a castle.

Princess Rosebud Project

Materials
- Buttons
- Coordinating patterned papers (samples provided on pages 46-47)
- Craft glue
- Scalloped edge scissors
- Scissors
- Scrapbook page

Instructions
Using the castle pattern on page 44, cut out all shapes with corresponding papers. Cut out openings for windows and doors. Use the cutouts for shutters and drawbridge.

Cut multiple strips in alternating patterned papers using scalloped edge scissors. Glue cut strips in alternating layers until you have the height of the rooftop patterns. (Tip: To prevent buckling, it helps to cut strips to 6" across.)

After you have a large enough section, cut out rooftops with patterns. Following castle pattern, mount and layer sections together on your background paper.

To make hinged doors and drawbridge, use ¼" strips of coordinating papers as hinges. Glue buttons to shutters and door to keep the doors closed and ease opening.

Castle Pattern

Princess Rosebud

Fairytale Clock

Because many of the scrapbook pages I have done are a labor of love, I try to find new ways to display them. A beautiful page filled with vintage images can be easily converted to a clock by using a kit available at craft stores.

Just to Dance

Just to dance—
just to let the music take you
in a way that seems to make you
feel suspended every time you leave the floor

Just to soar—
in a moment free and aerial
to rise magically ethereal
like an angel in a gossamary swirl

Just to Dance

My daughter, Olivia, has the heart of a romantic and an appreciation for dance. I photographed her in a series of dance moves, which creates a wonderful series on this page. Printing on vellum is a soft touch, especially when you want to add not detract.

Just to whirl—
And to nimbly pirouette
into a twirling silhouette
high on pointe, with muscles taught down to your toes...

Just to pose—
With body sculpted, statuesque
to execute and arabesque
and with fragile, artful grace sustain your stance...

Just to dance

~ by Linda Staten

Just to Whirl

Olivia has been the inspiration for many of my paintings, and I enjoy using the artwork like personal pictures on my scrapbook pages. Most photography software programs have tools to make photographs look like a watercolor or sketch.

Center Stage

Simple semi-circle patterns create this wonderful 20th-century stage embossed with stars for a dramatic effect and layered for dimension. The valance at top was stitched with a gold size 10 crochet thread using a simple backstitch kept very loose.

ADAM THE GREAT MAGICIAN

ABRACADABRA

JOKER

Hat Trick
My nephew is my King of Hearts and forever the joker. These family nicknames lovingly worked their way onto this page in the midst of a magic hat and wand.

In the Footlights

When I can't find the exact paper to suit a design idea, I embellish and create something custom.
Here a starburst hole punch was used, and a piece of gold cardstock was laid underneath.
Embossing details, such as the footlights on the stage, give the page dimension and texture.

Center Stage

Simple semi-circle patterns adorn this wonderful turn-of-the-last-century stage, which is embossed with
stars for a dramatic effect and layered for dimension.

Star Patterns

Hat Pattern

Chapter Three

Tea at Susan's

I have had more than 50 beautiful teas with several of my friends, and what always made them so unique were the special touches at each of the elaborately decorated tables.

Women notice, acknowledge, and appreciate all the details, which is why it's so fun to host themed tea parties. Party favors, place cards, handmade invitations, birthday cards, and handcrafted presents have made each tea a little "memory jewel."

Friendships honored in this way touch a woman's heart, and make for lovely memories that last a lifetime.

A Rose Tea

My painting "The Rose Room" inspired this Rose Tea page. Vintage cards on the invitation, beautiful ribbon stitching, and glass beads add decadent details. If you are pressed for time or want to watch expense, make one beautiful invitation, scan it, print out, and send to your guests.

A Rose Tea Lacing Project

Details such as lacing a page take extra time, but the results are well worth it. Even if you have had no experience doing needlework, you'll find these pages easy to embellish with lacing.

Materials
- Beads
- Decorative paper
- Hole punch
- Needle with large eye and thread
- Pencil
- Ribbon
- Ruler

Instructions
Make a guide on the back of your paper by making marks every 1" along the edge of the page. From those marks use a ruler and pencil to draw a grid of 1" blocks. Use a hole punch to make holes at each intersection. Make sure to use a needle with a large eye to ease threading of ribbon.

Stitching instructions: Beginning at A, bring needle and ribbon up through A and slide on bead. Go down through B, then come up through C and push needle through the bead. Go down through D. Repeat until you reach the end.

I prefer to have each of my pages interactive. I like to provide pages to open, or flaps to peek behind.

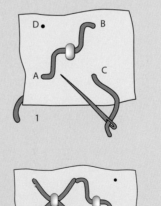

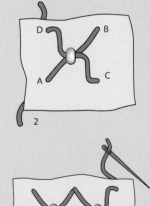

Rose Tea Tray

A tea tray is easy to make by adding handles to a wooden wall picture frame. Cabinet handles work best and can be attached by drilling holes in the frame and inserting screws through the underside.

Simple Solutions

Tea Tray Tips

- Use a wall frame; tabletop frames have an easel on the back and are not suitable for use as a tray.
- Use clear bathtub caulking around the edges of the glass where it meets the frame to keep spilled tea or other liquids from seeping onto the image.
- Add feet to the tray by inserting cabinet knobs. Use a two-sided screw to attach the feet.
- Finish the tray by gluing a piece of decorative paper over the back of the tray.

(Above, top right, and bottom right) The image for this tea tray has been layered for dimension. Make multiple copies of a picture and choose several elements that you would like to make dimensional. Use a craft knife to cut out several copies of those elements at a time and adhere them atop each other with foam squares.

Join Me for Tea Purse
Take tea on the road when you travel with a cigar box tea purse that's filled with everything you need to join a tea party.

Join Me for Tea Purse Interior
The inside of the tea purse holds a silver spoon, a special tea bag, and sweeteners. The box is lined with fabric, and ribbon is used to hold the items in place.

Join Me for Tea Purse Project

Materials
- ¼" batting
- Acrylic paint
- Decoupage medium
- Embellishments like lace, rub-on letters, and cut outs
- Hot glue gun
- Liquid bonding compound
- Purse handle
- Remnant fabric
- Ribbon
- Sandpaper, coarse
- Small sugar pouches
- Standard eyelets
- Teabag
- Thin cardboard
- Three teaspoons
- Wooden cigar box

Instructions
Purse Body
Disassemble and paint cigar box. For vintage look, paint dark base coat and a lighter top coat; let dry completely. Lightly sand with coarse sandpaper. Embellish outsides of box with images, lace, and desired text applied with a decoupage medium.

Hot glue ribbon in a crisscross design on the side, creating a lattice effect. Cut cardboard ¼" smaller than inside dimensions of all sides of cigar box. Layer with batting and cover with fabric using hot glue to secure.

Set eyelets for top inside insert and string ribbon through for holding spoon, tea, and sugar pouch. Hot glue fabric to inside of box.

Handle
Gently bend teaspoons back by heating them under very hot water. Wear gloves to protect hands from the heat. Attach spoons to purse handle using liquid bonding compound. Follow product instructions for dry time before working with handle.

When compound is set, reassemble cigar box and attach handle. Add tassels. Finish with lace, text, or decoupage cut outs.

Join Me for Tea

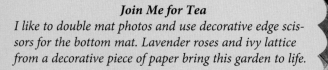

Join Me for Tea
I like to double mat photos and use decorative edge scissors for the bottom mat. Lavender roses and ivy lattice from a decorative piece of paper bring this garden to life.

A Special
Teatime Celebration!

_____
DATE

_____
TIME

_____
PLACE

_____
HOSTED BY

_____

But it is you...my close friend,
with whom I once enjoyed sweet fellowship.

THE BOOK OF PSALMS

Teatime Celebration
A publishing licensee designed special tea invitations, featuring one of my paintings on the cover and one on the inside, I used for a lavender-themed tea party.

Founder's Day Tea Tune

Sung to the tune of *Que Sera, Sera*

Jane's birthday, nineteen eithty-nine
Dear friend Fiona (she is so fine!)
Had an idea:
She'd host a tea
And she invited me!

It was such a treat!
We vowed that again we'd meet
To make each birthday such fun.
We had just begun!

To our Founder, praise
For her thoughtful ways.

Five years and fifty teas we've had.
Without our tea group, we'd be so sad.
Teas with fine presents,
Teas with great foods,
Teas with intriguing moods!

It is such a treat
Continuing still to meet.
Fiona inspired panache
(*Our* cakes have ganache!)

To our Founder, praise
For her clever ways.

Founder's Day Tea

My friend, Fiona, brought together a group of tea lovers several years ago. The words of a song commemorating our founder and a pullout fan with each member's portrait on the panels are fond memories of special times together. (Patterns for fan on page 69.)

A Founder's Day Tea or Fiona

Favorite Things
Photographs in frames, a pretty teacup, and a creative invitation designed like pullout paper dolls are favorite treasures from this fun occasion. (Pattern for invitation on page 70.)

Founder's Day Tea Fan Project

Materials
- Cardstock
- Heat embossing tools
- Hole punch
- Photographs
- Ribbon, thin
- Rivet
- Scanner and digital imaging software
- Scissors
- Tassel

Instructions
Using fan patterns on page 69, scan images and increase 15%. Using digital imaging software, import images of your friends and family and insert into center oval section of fan. Print as many as you need on cardstock. After printing, heat emboss small details on the fan blade to add texture and dimension. Cut out fan blades, center punch at bottom, and assemble with rivet. Attach ribbon at the back to keep fan together when closed. Add tassel.

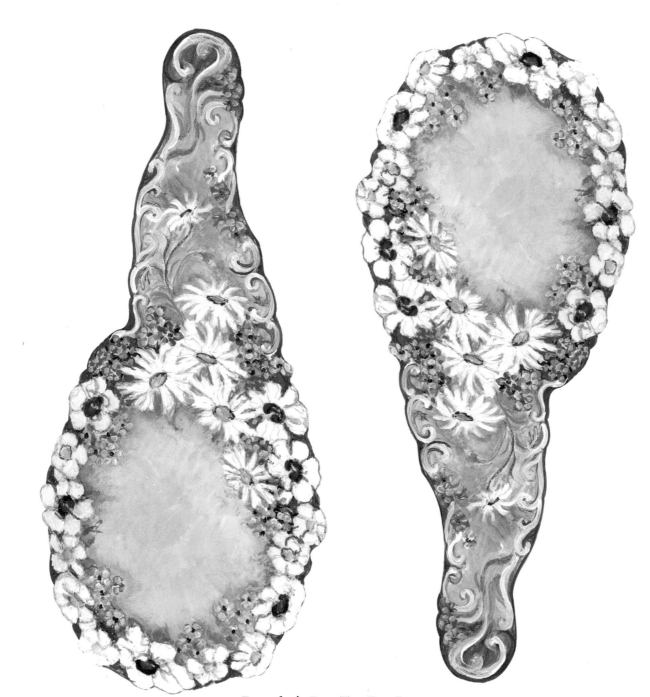

Founder's Day Tea Fan Patterns

Founder's Day Tea Invitation Pattern

Teacup Embellishment

A Literary Tea

OUR FAVORITE READINGS

Literary Tea in honour of Betsy's Birthday

MARK TWAIN
SHAKESPEARE
HEMINGWAY
CHARLES DICKENS

GARDENS

Reflections from a Woman Alone
A Lighthearted
at a Journey
Toward
Corinne Edwards

Literary Tea
My book club once held a tea themed after the great authors in literature. The invitation was a bookmark, and the favor was a compilation of our favorite quotes. These library books fold open to reveal precious images of a wonderful literary tea.

Chapter Four

Flowers from the Garden

Tranquil gardens are a common theme in my paintings, so it's no surprise that flowers and gardens inspired this chapter.

At a garden tea, I created "Seeds of Friendship" packets embellished with faces of my friends to use as place cards. Put into painted flowerpots, the packets could then be taken home by guests.

I used windows to illustrate looking out at your garden of friends, and I hand painted a paper to go with the flowerpots along a shuttered window, where photos of my friends were hung.

As you stroll down your garden path of memories, enjoy commemorating your seeds of friendship.

At the Window
I loved the idea of using foam core sheets to create my own window shutters hung with wide vintage ribbon. The key to making this type of page is to work with the sharpest craft blade possible.

Garden Window Shutters
Two long pieces of foam core cut into the shape of shutters,
complete with slats, create a great space to display favorite
mementos. Use miniature clothes pins to attach photographs.
(Pattern for shutter on page 76.)

Garden Window Shutters

Materials
- 8 ½" x 11" cardstock, 2 pieces
- Cardboard
- Craft glue
- Craft knife
- Decorative paper
- Foam squares
- Miniature clothes pins
- Pencil
- Photographs
- Ruler
- Thin cardboard

Instructions
Enlarge pattern 40%. For each shutter cut two 5" x 11" pieces of cardstock and one piece of cardboard the same size. Cover cardboard with decorative paper and craft glue. Using shutter pattern at right, measure 1" edge around, then draw horizontal lines 1" apart in the center on cardstock. Cut each horizontal line and ¾" on the sides with craft knife. Adhere to cardboard with glue and place foam squares under flap to raise (see photo above). Attach photos with miniature clothes pins.

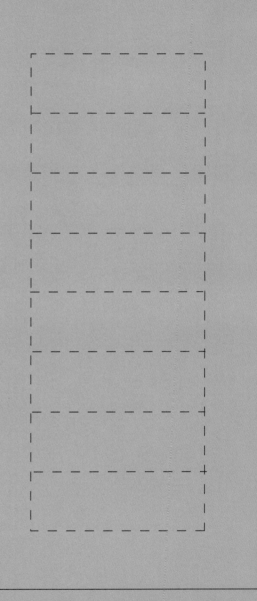

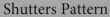
Shutters Pattern

I see a Garden
of Love grow

Garden Window
I enjoy taking a few moments each time I pass a window to look out and enjoy my garden. You can use the same pattern provided on the previous page to create a window page with a shutter that opens.

Garden Frame & Tea Box

I like to celebrate the joys of spring by making gifts for close friends. A frame blooming with flowers and a small box for storing tea are always welcome treasures.

Tea Box

(Right) A wooden craft or cigar box can be made into a lovely tea caddy. Decorate the outside of the box with delightful garden images and line the inside with fabric, or simply apply a coat of colorful paint. (Below) Adding an image of a colorful teacup inside of the box gives the project a little whimsy.

Garden Frame

(Right) Collect floral images from recycled greeting cards and adhere them to a wood frame with a decoupage medium. Don't be afraid to layer the images and let flowers peek out, much like in a cottage garden.

HOLLYHOCK

10¢

SUNFLOWER 10¢

DELPHINIUM

10¢

Seeds of Friendship

Seeds of Friendship

Cultivating friendships is my life's blood. What better way to get that point across than to have seed packets personalized for your closest friends? Grab a canvas gardener's bag and spade and you're ready to cultivate memories all year.

Seeds of Friendship Project

Materials
- Clear plastic sheet
- Craft glue
- Double-stick foam tape
- Photographs
- Plain cardstock
- Scissors
- Seeds

Instructions
Color photocopy seed patterns on this page or scan into your computer. If desired, add text to top of packet.

Cut out blank circle from seed patterns. Place clear plastic sheet on back to cover open circle. Cut plain cardstock same size as seed packet and edge with double-stick foam tape. Place picture in center and sprinkle a few seeds over it. Glue seed packet illustration onto cover.

Garden Setting
The Seeds of Friendship project inspired me to create a garden tea setting for friends. I had a delightful time with paint and brushes, decorating everything in sight!

Terra-cotta pots can be painted with acrylic craft paint. If you are intimidated at the thought of painting flowers, paint polka dots and decoupage a paper cutout of a rose on the outside of the pot.

The Seeds of Friendship project, which can be incorporated into table décor as plant picks, makes a wonderful take-home gift.

Paint designed for use on glass works well on ceramic plates. Your designs don't need to be elaborate; you may choose to paint a border or a simple flourish on the plates.

SEEDS OF

FRIENDSHIP

Chapter Five

Something to Celebrate

Holidays are wonderful times to commemorate on scrapbook pages. Family, traditions, and elements from each celebration offer a wealth of possibilities.

I love the old sugar panorama eggs and Easter baskets with big bows. The rich colors of Halloween and the beautiful photos of the family table at Thanksgiving were sources of inspiration for my pages.

Think about what you love best about each holiday and use those colors and ideas to embellish your pages.

Easter Chick

It's always fun to take pictures of one generation and match them up with photos from another. Deep chocolate color vintage ribbon, cards, and millinery flowers surround my granddaughter and her Easter chick.

Easter Greetings

Easter Basket
My love for panorama eggs inspired this Easter basket of memories featuring my daughter. Dimensional paint and glitter give a sugar-decorated effect while silk ribbons are woven to create the look of a treasured basket.

Basket Weave Project

Materials
- ½" ribbon
- 1" ribbon
- Cardstock
- Hot glue gun
- Scissors
- Tape

Instructions

Cut a half circle out of cardstock. Cover half circle, in diagonal pattern, with 1" ribbon, securing with tape on back. Weave ½" ribbons in opposite direction and secure to back with tape. For handle, use ¼" strip of cardstock wrapped in 1" ribbon and bend to form loop. Attach with hot glue gun on back of basket bottom.

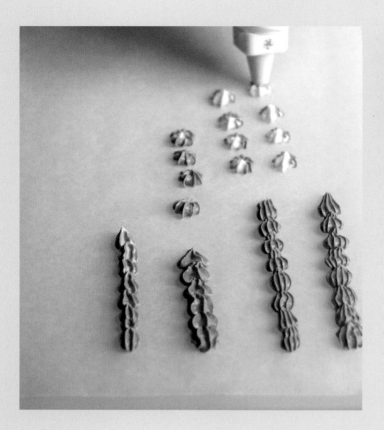

Sugaring Eggs Project

I discovered a product named Texture Magic while shopping in a craft store. It comes in many colors and is applied using decorative tips, much like those used for cake decorating.

I use a plastic cutting board to make shapes and designs to use on my scrapbook pages. I like to use two colors, which is easy to do by going over a design with a second color.

If I know exactly where I want my design, I apply it directly onto shapes cut from cardstock. I find multi-purpose paper too flimsy to work on. I vary tips to get a variety of textures. The compound comes out much like frosting does. While texture compound is still wet, sprinkle it with opalescent glitter. Vintage mica glitter works well too. Once compound is dry, it easily lifts off cutting board and can be glued directly onto page. Use a sharp craft knife to lift dimensional embellishments and put in place.

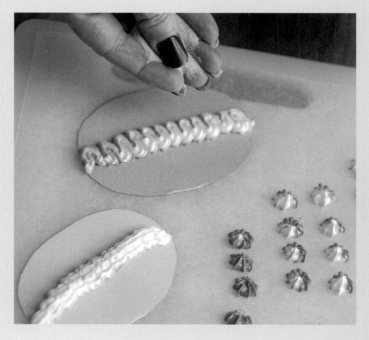

My Funny Valentine
Dogs truly are a woman's best friend. Bold colors and vintage valentines make the pages as special as my pets are to me.

My Funny Valentine
Sweet Comic Valentine

Benny

To my Love

You Make Me Smile With My Heart ♥

To my Valentine

June

You Make Me Smile
I really felt like I was able to express my true personality in these valentine pages. Don't be afraid of color. Cropping the shots of the dogs tight lets their cute expressions dominate the page.

Trick or Treat,
Fiona 1999

Happy Halloween

Happy Halloween

Happy Halloween
*An elegant black-and-gold theme is more my style for Halloween.
Vintage doilies with pierced edges and velvet leaves in fall colors
add richness to this wonderful childhood fantasy holiday.*

Halloween
is
So Much Fun!
Oct. 31,
1998

A Halloween Beauty

A soft sheer fabric with gold stars is a nice background for memories of the year Rosie was Snow White for Halloween. The witch's hat is made from vintage paper and a gold doily.

Circle of Family

Giving thanks for family and harvest is the theme of this family portrait around the Thanksgiving table. Who says a portrait has to be square? Make it into the shape of a pumpkin and nestle it among vintage ribbons and leaves.

Autumn Memories

Cut photos of friends and family into shapes such as a pumpkin and place them on any background you wish. This will ensure a cohesive page thanks to the similar color choices, even if the photos were taken at different times.

Layers of fall leaves are made by cutting shapes in a variety of autumn colors and decorating some with gold embossing powder and others with small green glass beads. Bend each leaf slightly to give the leaves some dimension.

Small millinery decorations such as pearl berries add elegance to a page of thankful memories.

Lace cutouts can be used for borders and matting. Look for pieces at flea markets and consignment stores.

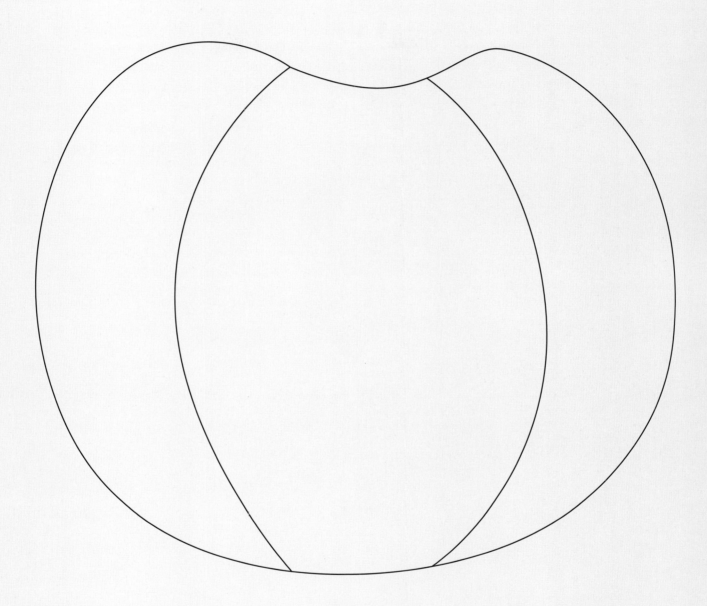

Pumpkin Pattern

Chapter Six

Christmas Treasures

Christmas stories and gingerbread houses are two long-standing traditions in my family. An image from one of my paintings was the perfect background paper for creating my version of "The Night Before Christmas."

Using your family name and photos would make a great page for your family album, and copies could even be given as gifts.

The gingerbread house I made was sheer fun using dimensional paint as the icing trim. The color, texture, and magic that are Christmas, coupled with favorite photos, offer endless possibilities for making pages merry and bright.

Night Before Christmas
Matching words with pictures is the key to bringing your own family story to life. The background paper for these pages was made by flopping one image on the computer and mounting them as mirror images. You can copy the images on pages 106–107 for your background.

stockings were hung
by the chimney with care . . .

in hopes that St. Nich...
soon would b...

Night Before Christmas Accordion Project

Materials
- Acrylic paint, gold
- Cardstock, cranberry
- Craft glue
- Embossing tool
- Fairy dust
- Fine-tip pen
- Holly images
- Photographs
- Pre-made accordion book
- Scissors

Instructions
Make color copies of the Night Before Christmas accordion book pages (pages 103-105). Cut out blank spaces for your photographs and glue selected photos that match the storylines onto the back. Attach the pages to a small pre-made accordion book available at most craft supply retailers.

Create a cover with cranberry cardstock, embellished with holly images on the sides for "hinges," and embossed with fairy dust. Write the title and emboss with gold paint. We've included two sets of blank book pages so you can make an Accordion book to keep and to give.

T'was the night before Christmas . . .

T'was the night before Christmas . . .

and all through the house . . .

and all through the house . . .

Accordion Book Pages

Accordion Book Pages

The stockings were hung
by the chimney with care . . .

The stockings were hung
by the chimney with care . . .

in hopes that St. Nicholas
soon would be there.

in hopes that St. Nicholas
soon would be there.

Accordion Book Pages

For SANTA

SusanRios

Mom and Dad 1995

Christmas with Mom & Dad
The Christmas family portrait is a cherished tradition in our family. Elegant glittered and embossed paper, holly, red roses, and ribbons surround this festive photo of my parents.

Santa Box & Frame

These two projects are quick and fun. A wood photo frame and box are painted black. Images are cut out and adhered using a decoupage medium. After the projects are dry, you can use embossing powder for more decoration. The following pages contain images to photocopy and use.

Scrapbooking Embellishments

Scrapbooking Embellishments

Scrapbooking Embellishments

Scrapbooking Embellishments

Gingerbread House Project

Materials
- Cardstock: 1 sheet each of red, pink, white, blue, brown
- Craft glue
- Dimensional paint: Spring Green, White, Country Red, Raspberry
- Dimensional paint tips
- Gumdrops
- Marshmallows
- Scissors
- White glitter

Instructions
Assemble gingerbread house background with red, pink, white, and blue papers. Cut simple house shape out of brown cardstock. Glue to background with white paper "snow" base. Apply white dimensional paint with fine tip, starting with the roof, creating diamond shapes and small icicles along the roofline. Outline windows and doors, and make swirls in empty spaces, giving it that candy house feel.

Switch to Country Red without cleaning tip, which will help create variegated color accents on roof and borders.

Switch to star tip and Spring Green and Raspberry dimensional paints to create the winter trees. When you are finished with dimensional paint accents, sprinkle entire surface with glitter and allow to dry overnight.

After dimensional paint dries, turn gingerbread house over to remove excess glitter and finish embellishing with marshmallow snowman and gumdrop stepping stones (both available at your local crafts store).

Gingerbread House

One of my favorite family projects during the holidays is crafting gingerbread houses, which served as the inspiration for creating a gingerbread house page. Paper, texture, and glitter make this house sparkle.

Gingerbread Gift Tags
Brown cardstock is used for the background of the gingerbread gift tag and matching gift box. The gift box can be used over and over. The same texture compound was used for the snow as was used on the gingerbread house.

Family Christmas Cookies
Food plays an important role in many of our family traditions. Favorite recipes are showcased in a small folded book filled with cookie recipes. The cover of the book is decorated with texture cookies and goodies.

Chapter Seven

Work in Progress

The first two pages in this chapter celebrate my career as an artist. I think it would be wonderful to acknowledge someone you love by creating a scrapbook page honoring his or her contribution to the world.

The rest of the pages throughout this chapter offer ways to personalize a workspace. Whether it's for a working woman or stay-at-home mom, something beautiful on our desk would be appreciated by every one of us.

The things I made might give you some ideas for little treasures you can create for your own desk, or a lovely gift for someone special.

A Canvas of Love
In creating pages of memories don't overlook your own accomplishments. Your hobbies, interests, and even your career can be beautifully crafted into an heirloom that you can enjoy for many years. Images you can copy and use are on pages 122-125.

A Brush with Romance

A Brush with Romance

I created these pages to celebrate my 27-year career as an artist. Perhaps these pages may help you celebrate an artist you know or help to bring out the artist in you.

Scrapbooking Embellishment

Scrapbooking Embellishment

Scrapbooking Embellishment

Scrapbooking Embellishments

Gift From the Heart Card

Personal, handmade gifts are cherished the most in my home. This is a gift that keeps on giving. A small canvas crafted into a scrap-book page was scanned and note cards were made with the image.

The recipient of this gift will find a surprise inside: a set of thank-you notes tucked in the back of the canvas.

I combined all of my favorite details in this special canvas. I used vintage ribbon, millinery flowers, ephemera, crystals, and texture compound with glitter.

Gift From the Heart Card Project

Materials
- 8" x 10" canvas
- Computer and scanner
- Embellishments
- Paper
- Ribbon

Instructions

Create scrapbook page on 8" x 10" canvas using your favorite embellishments. Scan finished canvas, then use this image to create 4" x 6" gift cards on your computer. If your finished "page" has a lot of depth, a digital photograph works well too. The gift cards nest nicely between the stretcher bars on the back of the canvas. Tie a ribbon around the canvas to keep everything together nicely for gift giving

Two pearl buttons suggest the wings of my heart.

Accordion File Folder Project

Materials
- Acrylic paint
- Cardstock
- Craft glue
- Embellishments
- Hook-and-loop tape
- Hot glue gun
- Manila folders
- Ribbon
- Scissors
- Scrapbooking embellishments
- Two 8" x 10" canvases

Instructions

Cover inside of two 8" x 10" canvases with sturdy piece of card-stock of your choice. Paint outside and embellish as you would any scrapbook page.

Hot glue piece of ribbon to backside of one of canvases. Attach ribbon at front with hook-and-loop tape and tie into bow to keep folder closed when not in use.

Cut manila folders down to 7" x 9", then adhere to each other with craft glue. Attach folders to inside of front and back covers with craft glue. Hot glue end folders to back of canvases.

Accordion File Folder

Making a creative space of your own doesn't stop with floors and walls. I like to have a special place to keep some of the scraps I work with. This personalized accordion file folder is perfect for cataloging and keeping small pieces organized.

Something Old, Something New

This was one of my favorite pages. I loved using scans of my heirloom handkerchiefs as borders and backgrounds to accent my parents' wedding portrait. By showcasing a treasured family photo, you create a lasting keepsake.

Something Borrowed, Something Blue
Vintage millinery flowers and pearl accents provide the ideal finishing touches on this page commemorating a cherished family moment. Try to find a similar type of flower or colors in the photograph to tie the various elements together.

Family Story
A photograph of my parents' wedding (above) serves as the cover of a mini-album that tells our family story. (Right) My sister and I are shown with my father in our Sunday best. An addition like this makes a page more than a single memory—it conveys history.

Our new dolls ♥

Your heart carries beauty into the World

Treasure Chest
Some women may consider a jewelry box a treasure chest, but for me true gems are vintage lace, ribbons, trims, and papers. I painted this small chest of drawers so I would have a special place to keep my personal treasures. You could also cover the chest with decorative paper.

From the Author

The Pleasure was Mine

When I started working on this book, I had no idea I would become completely consumed by scrapbooking. There was no way I would have guessed I would become so enraptured with the details and beauty of working with so many of my favorite materials.

I now know first-hand how enjoyable it can be, and I understand why this market is growing to be larger than anyone could have predicted.

There is something so personally gratifying about spending time with your memories, creating something for future generations to see. It is a pause in a busy world to count blessings and become committed to, and more aware of, happy memories in the making.

We are all artists in our own way. I hope the projects throughout this book inspire you and give you the motivation to find your own personal creativity. I hope you'll make a date with the artist within and spend a moment or two counting your own blessings while scrapbooking.

I invite you to browse through my Gallery of Paintings on the following pages. I hope they inspire you to create your own fanciful scrapbook pages for your own projects.

Sarah

SusanRios

Thank You

Thank You

Gallery of Paintings

Attic Memories

Be Mine

Breath of Spring

Celebrate Life

Christmas Treasures

Cozy Christmas Memories

Gallery of Paintings

Enchanted Christmas

Finding the Meaning

Freedom Way

Garden Terrace

Grateful for Home

Holiday Tea

Gallery of Paintings

Journey of the Heart

The Joy of Christmas

The Magic of Christmas

Morning Discovery

Notes

Partners in Play

Gallery of Paintings

Paulette's Corner

Pheobe

The Porch

The Rose Room

The Sitting Room

Spring Tea

Gallery of Paintings

A Sweet Remembrance

Tea at Summer Hill

Tea at Susan's

Theodore

Victorian Christmas

Work in Progress

Credits

Book Editor: Eileen Paulin
Copy Editor: Catherine Risling
Stylists: Rebecca Ittner
         Jayne Cosh
Photographers: Zac Williams
         Denny Nelson
Book Designer: Brenda Rogers
         Pinnacle Marketing
         Ogden, UT

A Special Thanks

Thank you Eileen Paulin and Jo Packham for being my friends, appreciating my art, and giving me the support to expand my talents into the scrapbooking arena.

Thank you Mike Snow for working side-by-side with me on this project, and for contributing your wonderful ideas, your incredible talent, and your unsurpassed computer skills.

A heartfelt thank you to my friend and business partner, Greg Johnsen, for supporting me in every way throughout this project, and for being a source of inspiration.

Thank you to the best team of people anyone could ever work with: R. J. Booker, Carol Dyer, Dawn Dorn, and last but not least Beverly Bruce, whose motto I whole-heartedly endorse, "When in doubt . . . overdo!"

Acknowledgments

3M/Scotch
www.3m.com

Delta
Texture Magic Dimensional Paint
www.deltacrafts.com

DMD Industries
www.dmdind.com

Dolls and Lace
www.DollsandLace.com

K&Company
www.kandcompany.com

Making Memories
www.makingmemories.com

Offray
www.offray.com

The Paper Rabbit
www.paperrabbit.com

Paris to the Moon
Costa Mesa, CA

Provo Craft & Novelty, Inc.
www.provocraft.com

Stamp Your Heart Out
www.stampyourheartout.com

Stampendous! Inc.
www.stampendous.com

Susan Rios, Inc.
www.susanriosinc.com

Uchida of America, Corp.
www.uchida.com

Victori-ana
Montrose, CA

Metric Equivalency Charts

inches to millimeters and centimeters

inches	mm	cm	inches	cm	inches	cm
⅛	3	0.3	9	22.9	30	76.2
¼	6	0.6	10	25.4	31	78.7
½	13	1.3	12	30.5	33	83.8
⅝	16	1.6	13	33.0	34	86.4
¾	19	1.9	14	35.6	35	88.9
⅞	22	2.2	15	38.1	36	91.4
1	25	2.5	16	40.6	37	94.0
1¼	32	3.2	17	43.2	38	96.5
1½	38	3.8	18	45.7	39	99.1
1¾	44	4.4	19	48.3	40	101.6
2	51	5.1	20	50.8	41	104.1
2½	64	6.4	21	53.3	42	106.7
3	76	7.6	22	55.9	43	109.2
3½	89	8.9	23	58.4	44	111.8
4	102	10.2	24	61.0	45	114.3
4½	114	11.4	25	63.5	46	116.8
5	127	12.7	26	66.0	47	119.4
6	152	15.2	27	68.6	48	121.9
7	178	17.8	28	71.1	49	124.5
8	203	20.3	29	73.7	50	127.0

yards to meters

yards	meters	yards	meters	yards	meters	yards	meters	yards	meters
⅛	0.11	2⅛	1.94	4⅛	3.77	6⅛	5.60	8⅛	7.43
⅛	0.11	2⅛	1.94	4⅛	3.77	6⅛	5.60	8⅛	7.43
¼	0.23	2¼	2.06	4¼	3.89	6¼	5.72	8¼	7.54
⅜	0.34	2⅜	2.17	4⅜	4.00	6⅜	5.83	8⅜	7.66
⅝	0.46	2½	2.29	4½	4.11	6½	5.94	8½	7.77
⅝	0.57	2⅝	2.40	4⅝	4.23	6⅝	6.06	8⅝	7.89
¾	0.69	2¾	2.51	4¾	4.34	6¾	6.17	8¾	8.00
⅞	0.80	2⅞	2.63	4⅞	4.46	6⅞	6.29	8⅞	8.12
1	0.91	3	2.74	5	4.57	7	6.40	9	8.23
1¼	1.03	3¼	2.86	5⅛	4.69	7¼	6.52	9⅛	8.34
1¼	1.14	3¼	2.97	5¼	4.80	7¼	6.63	9¼	8.46
1⅜	1.26	3⅜	3.09	5⅜	4.91	7⅜	6.74	9⅜	8.57
1½	1.37	3½	3.20	5½	5.03	7½	6.86	9½	8.69
1⅝	1.49	3⅝	3.31	5⅝	5.14	7⅝	6.97	9⅝	8.80
1¾	1.60	3¾	3.43	5¾	5.26	7¾	7.09	9¾	8.92
1⅞	1.71	3⅞	3.54	5⅞	5.37	7⅞	7.20	9⅞	9.03
2	1.83	4	3.66	6	5.49	8	7.32	10	9.14

Index